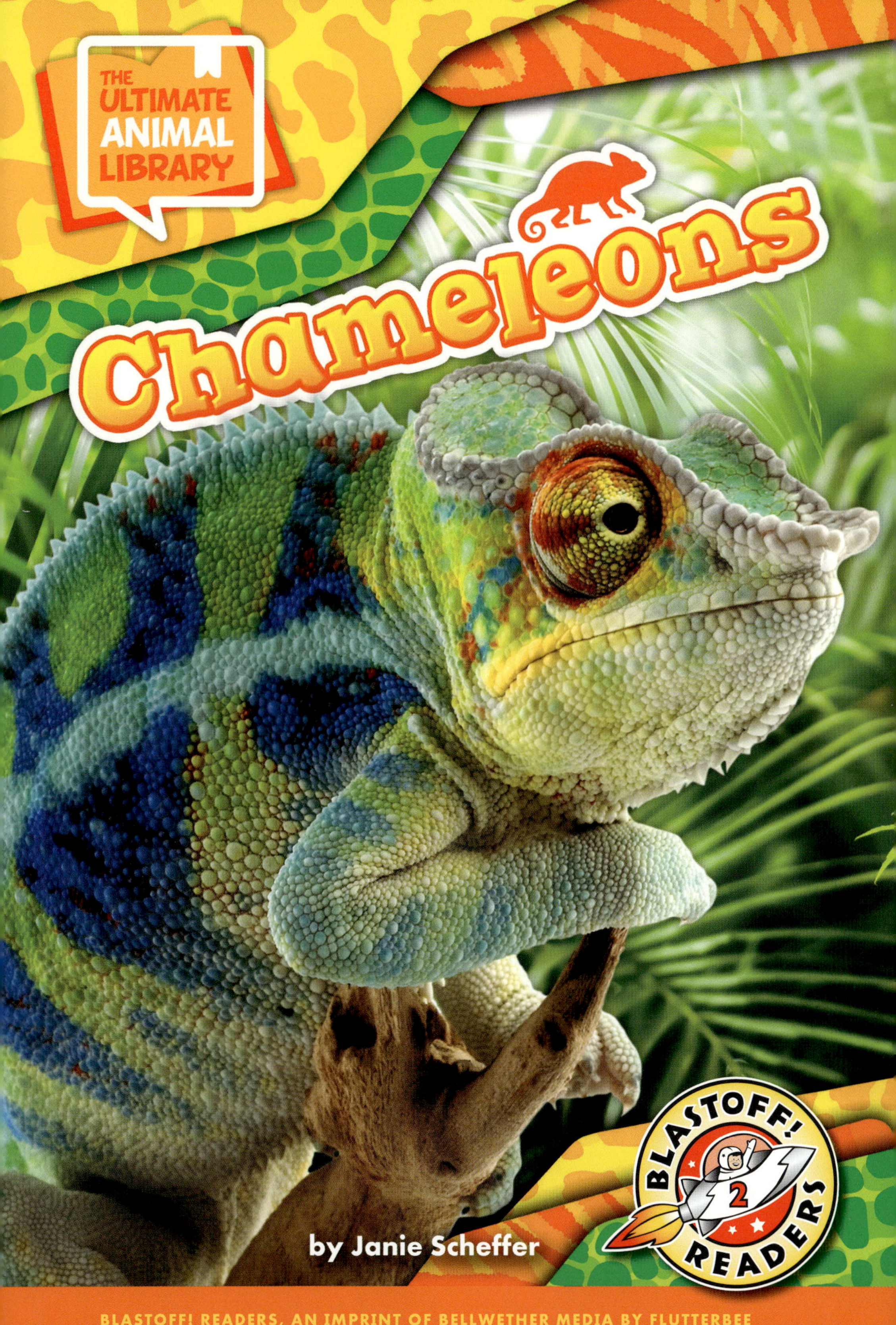

BLASTOFF! READERS, AN IMPRINT OF BELLWETHER MEDIA BY FLUTTERBEE

Blastoff! Readers are carefully developed by literacy experts to build reading stamina and move students toward fluency by combining standards-based content with developmentally appropriate text.

LEVELS

Level 1 provides the most support through repetition of high-frequency words, light text, predictable sentence patterns, and strong visual support.

Level 2 offers early readers a bit more challenge through varied sentences, increased text load, and text-supportive special features.

Level 3 advances early-fluent readers toward fluency through increased text load, less reliance on photos, advancing concepts, longer sentences, and more complex special features.

★ **Blastoff! Universe**

Reading Level

Blastoff! Beginners	Blastoff! Readers	Blastoff! Discovery
Grade K	Grades 1–3	Grade 4

This edition first published in 2026 by Bellwether Media, Inc.

For information regarding permission, write to Bellwether Media, Inc., Attention: Permissions Department, 3500 American Blvd W, Suite 150, Bloomington, MN 55431.

Library of Congress Cataloging-in-Publication Data is available at www.loc.gov or upon request from the publisher.

ISBN: 9798893047912 (hardcover)
ISBN: 9798893048919 (ebook)

Editor: Elizabeth Neuenfeldt Designer: Brittany McIntosh

Printed in the United States of America, North Mankato, MN.

Table of Contents

What Are Chameleons?

Chameleons are **reptiles**. There are over 200 **species**! They live in Africa, Asia, and Europe. Many species live in Madagascar.

Mediterranean Chameleon Report

Status in the Wild

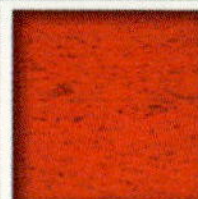

least concern

Habitats

deserts

forests

savannas

Chameleons can be different sizes. The longest are 27 inches (68.6 centimeters) long.

The shortest are less than
1 inch (2.5 centimeters) long!

Chameleons are often green or brown.

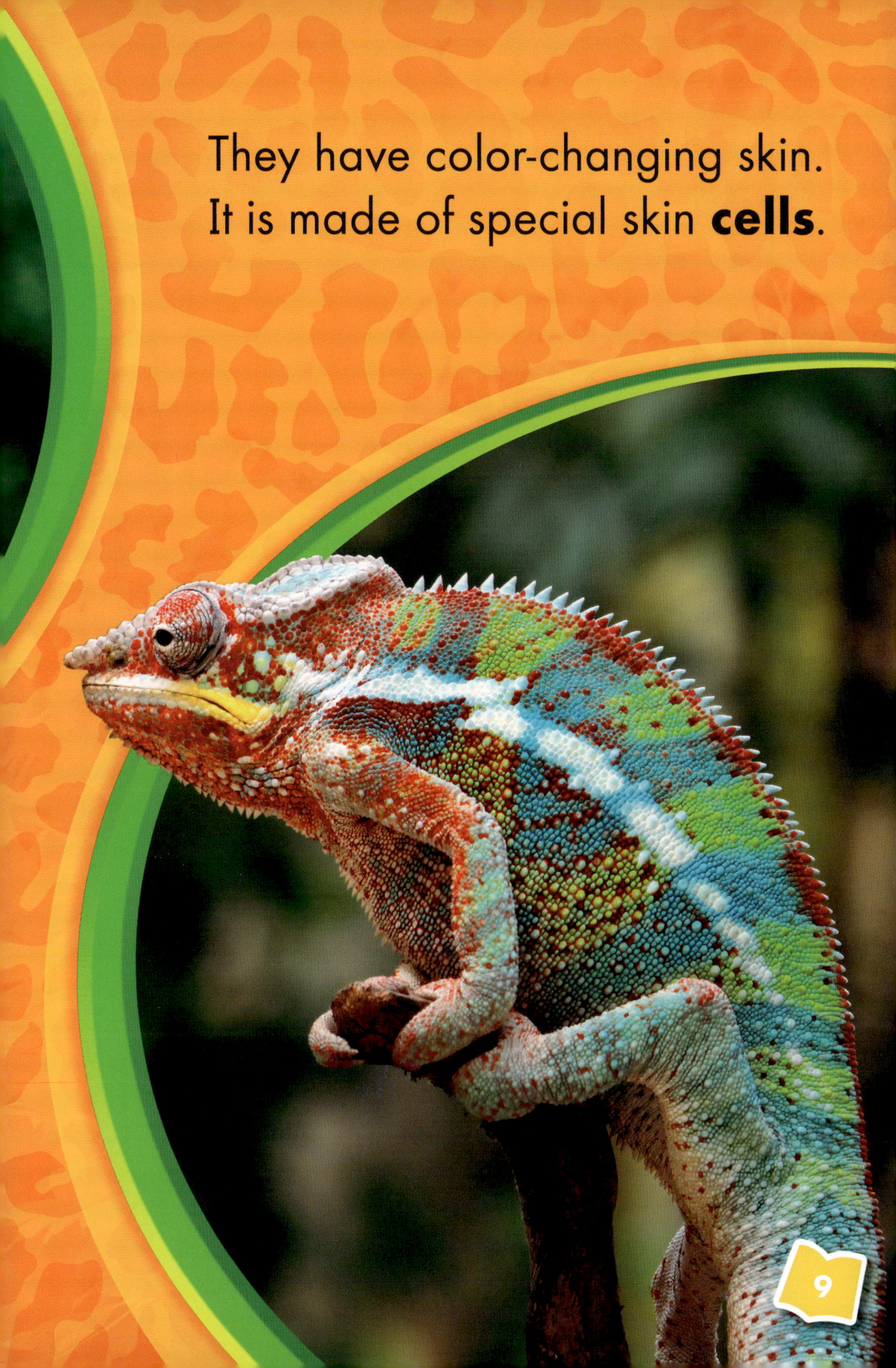

They have color-changing skin.
It is made of special skin **cells**.

Chameleons have **bulging** eyes. Their eyes can move in different directions at once.

They have long, sticky tongues. They easily catch **prey**. Some chameleons have horns.

Spot a Chameleon

bulging eyes

color-changing skin

long, sticky tongue

tongue

Hidden Hunters

Chameleons live in many **habitats**. They often live in trees or bushes. They live alone.

During the day, they hunt and lie in the sun. They do not move far.

Chameleons eat mostly **insects**.
Some also eat plants or birds.

They wait and watch for prey. They quickly stick out their tongues to catch it!

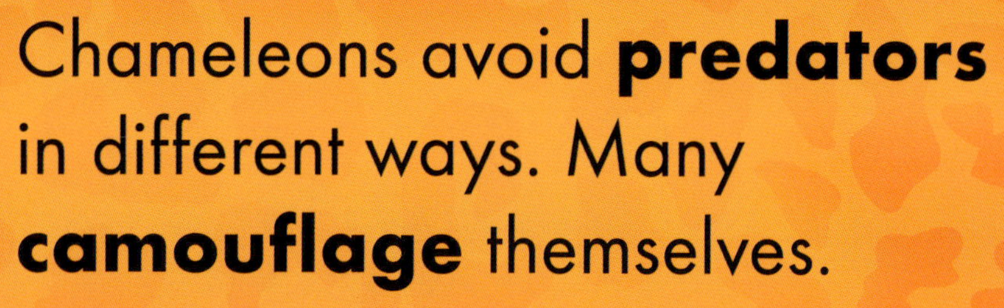

Chameleons avoid **predators** in different ways. Many **camouflage** themselves.

Others may run away or fight back. Some species even play dead!

Growing Up

Most female chameleons lay eggs. They bury their eggs to keep them safe.

The eggs **hatch** 4 to 24 months later. **Hatchlings** come out. They look like tiny adult chameleons.

hatchling

eggs

Chameleon hatchlings live on their own right away. They soon begin hunting insects.

About one year later, chameleons become adults. Most live for about nine years!

Life of a Chameleon

Name of Babies

hatchlings

Number of Eggs

2 to 80

Time Spent in Eggs

4 to 24 months

Life Span

Glossary

bulging—standing out from something

camouflage—to blend in with surroundings

cells—the smallest units of living things

habitats—places where animals live

hatch—to break open

hatchlings—baby chameleons

insects—small animals with six legs and bodies divided into three parts

predators—animals that hunt other animals for food

prey—animals that are hunted by other animals for food

reptiles—cold-blooded animals that have backbones and usually lay eggs

species—kinds of an animal

To Learn More

AT THE LIBRARY

Gendell, Megan. *Chameleons.* Mendota Heights, Minn.: Apex, 2024.

Slade, Suzanne. *Behold the Chameleon.* Atlanta, Ga.: Peachtree, 2025.

Weakland, Mark. *Chameleons.* Mankato, Minn.: Black Rabbit Books, 2024.

ON THE WEB

FACTSURFER

Factsurfer.com gives you a safe, fun way to find more information.

1. Go to www.factsurfer.com.
2. Enter "chameleons" into the search box and click 🔍.
3. Select your book cover to see a list of related content.

Index

The images in this book are reproduced through the courtesy of: fivespots, front cover (chameleon); winyuu, front cover (background), pp. 2-3; Kurit afshen, pp. 3, 9, 11 (tongue); Christoph Bosch/ Alamy Stock Photo, p. 4; imageBROKER.com GmbH & Co. KG/ Alamy Stock Photo, p. 6; MadeleinWolf/ Alamy Stock Photo, p. 7; Lauren Suryanata, p. 8; Gaschwald, p. 10; Tanto Yensen, pp. 10-11; Eric Isselee, pp. 11 (chameleon), 23; Dennis van de Water, p. 12; GarryKillian/ Alamy Stock Photo, p. 13; SimonSkafar, pp. 14-15; FJAH, p. 15 (birds); SpaceLay, p. 15 (rats); Dan_Koleska, p. 15 (snakes); Vera Larina, p. 15 (chameleon); piemags/ nature/ Alamy Stock Photo, p. 15 (beetles); Macronatura.es, p. 15 (grasshoppers); Paco Moreno, p. 15 (crickets); Nature Picture Library/ Alamy Stock Photo, p. 16; Lorne Chapman/ Alamy Stock Photo, p. 17; Nick Henn, p. 18; COULANGES, pp. 18-19; RZ_Images/ Alamy Stock Photo, p. 20; Lillian King/ Getty Images, p. 21.